SONNETS WITH TWO TORCHES AND ONE CLIFF

Books by Robert Thomas

Door to Door
Dragging the Lake
Bridge
Sonnets with Two Torches and One Cliff

SONNETS WITH TWO TORCHES AND ONE CLIFF

Robert Thomas

Carnegie Mellon University Press
Pittsburgh 2023

ACKNOWLEDGMENTS

I wish to thank the editors of the following publications in which these poems or versions of them first appeared:

The Antioch Review: "Sonnet with Venison and Frigg"; *Atlanta Review*: "Sonnet with Warm Milk and Shovel," "Sonnet with Sign and Romansch Languages"; *Barrow Street*: "Sonnet with Blowtorch and Brat," "Sonnet with Toothpick and Street Fair"; *Beloit Poetry Journal*: "Sonnet with Abalone and Glue," "Sonnet with Goldfish and Proxima Centauri," "Sonnet with Rain Dance and Gitanes"; *California Quarterly*: "Sonnet with Slings and Sliders"; *Catamaran*: "Sonnet with Taqueria and Fishtail"; *Cumberland River Review*: "Sonnet with Ribs and Obelisk," "Sonnet with Zinc and Rhododendrons"; *DMQ Review*: "Sonnet with Two Torches and One Cliff"; *FIELD*: "Sonnet with Backpack and Jack," "Sonnet with Mozart and Bear"; *The Georgia Review*: "Sonnet with Ham and Rose"; *Hotel Amerika*: "Sonnet with Blizzard and Glass Lizard," "Sonnet with Post-its and Johnny Depp," "Sonnet with Storm Drain and Thyme"; *The Massachusetts Review*: "Sonnet with Ghost Writer and Syringe"; *New Ohio Review*: "Sonnet with Hound and Sequins," "Sonnet with Acne and Hawk"; *Nimrod International Journal*: "Sonnet with Aioli and Roux," "Sonnet with Clerk and Genghis Khan," "Negligee and Hatchet: A Sonnet Crown," "Sonnet with Blackberries and Clocks," "Sonnet with Sump and Sourdough," "Sonnet with Seashell and Chinatown," "Sonnet with Ark and Tug," "Sonnet with Vespers and Machine Tools," "Sonnet with Ochre and Aurochs," "Sonnet with Jokes and Car Jack," "Sonnet with Barn Dance and Solar Storm," "Sonnet with Squeegee and Cracker Jack," "Sonnet with Zombie and Zoot Suit," "Sonnet Without Jukebox or Fox," "Sonnet with Hard Rain and Spreadsheet," "Sonnet with Velvet and Buck," "Sonnet with Oak and Aspen," "Sonnet with Negligee and Hatchet"; *North American Review*: "Sonnet with Jury and Sunset"; *Omnium Gatherum Quarterly*: "Sonnet with Ice Hockey and Night Goggles," "Sonnet with Lobster and Priest"; *One*: "Sonnet with Blue Sphere and Ruby, My Dear"; *Phoebe*: "Sonnet with Emergency Room and Skillet"; *Pleiades*: "Sonnet with Used Car and Julia Child"; *Poet Lore*: "Sonnet with Maenad and Kiln"; *RHINO Poetry*: "Sonnet with Schlock and Yonder"; *River Styx*: "Sonnet with Hedge Fund and Trout," "Sonnet with Q-tip and Fugue"; *Southern Indiana Review*: "Sonnet with Jackhammer and ACLU," "Sonnet with Sappho and Wrecking Yard"; *The Southern Review*: "Sonnet with Juicer and Prism"; *Subtropics*: "Sonnet with Mud and Pillow," "Sonnet with Oven and Green Nets," "Sonnet with Sword and Petticoat," "Sonnet with Zipper and Bioluminescence"; *Sugar House Review*: "Sonnet with Death and Red-Checked Tablecloth"; *TriQuarterly*: "Sonnet with Quartz and Rice"; *Valparaiso Poetry Review*: "Sonnet with Purgatory and Scratch"; *The Yale Review*: "Sonnet with Fish and Bayonet," "Sonnet with Splinters and Veronicas," "Sonnet with Swan and Long Tall Sally"; *ZYZZYVA*: "Sonnet with Mouth and Stone."

"Negligee and Hatchet: A Sonnet Crown" was chosen by Kim Addonizio for first prize in the 2019 *Nimrod International Journal* Pablo Neruda Prize for Poetry.

"Sonnet with Mozart and Bear" was featured on *Verse Daily* on November 28, 2018.

"Sonnet with Taqueria and Fishtail" was featured as Poem of the Day by San Francisco Public Library on March 8, 2021.

Book design by Martina Rethman

Library of Congress Control Number 2022943608
ISBN 978-0-88748-691-3

10 9 8 7 6 5 4 3 2 1

for Cheryl

I gathered the jasmine your footsteps left behind.

—Pablo Neruda, "Soneto de Amor LVII"

CONTENTS

Of all forms of impossibility, the arrow strikes us into triangles to such an extraordinary extent that this phenomenon must be examined for its creative role in soul-making. . . . So necessary is the triangular pattern that, even where two exist only for each other, a third will be imagined.

—James Hillman, "On Psychological Creativity"

"O whaten a mountain is yon," she said,
"All so dreary wi' frost and snow?"
"O yon is the mountain of hell," he cried,
"Where you and I will go."

—Anonymous, "The Daemon Lover," or, "The House Carpenter"

SONNET WITH BACKPACK AND JACK

For your big day I bake you a Betty
Crocker. Jack toasts a brioche he roughed up,
then stuffed deep in his brick oven. I haul
a haiku, awkward as a whale, ashore
for you. Jack sings you an opera he wrote
on the green back of his backpack on BART,
jamming Mozart and Trent Reznor's best riffs
into a third thing, the music *music*
would make for itself, if it had his hands.
I burn cedar logs in a granite hearth.
Jack sets your house on fire, then sprawls with you
on wet grass till the heat hits the flash point,
your eyes widen, everything widens and
I am white thread lost in the night's wide eye.

SONNET WITHOUT MARK OR MANGER

I even forged the nails with my own hands.
Now she wants me to build a cedar bed,
not for us of course—for him, his divine
baby fat. Oh, I can do it: one stroke
of my hammer is all it takes to drive
a nail through. It's tempting to hit it so
precisely it pierces the wood enough
to graze his holy head but not break skin.
He'd grow up with a hankering for hot
iron, its harrowing kiss. Sacred freak!
A constant reminder my virgin wife
knows what it is to know God, the searching
lunge of his tongue. All I can do is watch
him slobber, gorge, and grow large at her breast.

SONNET WITH MOZART AND BEAR

Whoever you're with, I'm sure he's the real
deal, the pith of the myth, a fanged Wolfgang
to my toothless Salieri. Your unsheathed
claws never exhaust his mahogany
scratching post. He can overhaul the night
and underwrite its darkness while you wait.
Your ram pens *Hamlet* for his restless ewe.
I hem and haw with the mule in the barn.
"Sometimes I just want a man who *does* things,"
you say. Maybe I should kill a grizzly,
fuck the Thou out of your whiz kid's sublime
I-Thou. Jazz like that. When I say "I *do*
things too," a silence falls. Scarlet embers
of a thousand angels flare and perish.

SONNET WITH GOLDFISH
AND PROXIMA CENTAURI

You ask what Jack I could be jealous of.
Of the white rose, how the muted spatters
of rain conjure pink spots on its petals,
as if faint bloodstains appeared on the page
when you held a poem over a flame;
of the black moor goldfish and how it glides
effortlessly through rough limestone grottoes;
of hydrogen, its flammability
and abundance; of the long migration
of monarchs, their winters in Mexico,
how the ones who begin it aren't the ones
who end it, like the three generations
that it would take to reach the nearest star,
those astronauts anything but homesick.

SONNET WITH BLOWTORCH AND BRAT

Angel: acetylene blowtorch of grief,
zeal, frenzy *and* the slow glacier that sheared
Half Dome's granite hull, showing no mercy
to God for those who drowned in his wake. No
love, no bliss, is wilder than a mother's
for her brat, her broth of greed, noise and goo.
The genius of God is to imitate
the child, to be the ore the blast furnace
of the angel's love smelts, turning the pig
iron of God to steel. God makes himself
an empty field so we can dance on him.
He *is* the North, where the wolves howl for joy
to roam the vacant snow that offers them
no warmth, no meat, no blood, no fire, no love.

SONNET WITH STEPMOTHER
AND FLYING HORSES

What was it like for my mom to come home
to find my dad in bed with Jan, the next
wife, who would in her turn be succeeded
by #5? He'd have laughed. Not at her,
he wasn't *that* cruel, but at the scene.
I get my sense of the absurd from him.
He would have laughed if *he'd* walked in on *her*.
In that instant she saw all that would come:
the smoke-blue suit Jan wore for the wedding,
hair coiled in a French twist for the glad day;
Jan showing me how to stand and topple
dominoes, the most fun I'd ever had;
Jan taking me on a merry-go-round—
my first—not watching, riding by my side.

SONNET WITH NEON AND LAMB

Who are you with now, my bail-bond angel,
my flush blood bank? Your flashing neon sign
blinks Cash: No Questions Asked to every Tom,
Lick and Marry. You're quick as a live wire,
quiet as dew. Love me, fever me, be-
reave me. Please, true-blue Penelope, weave
me into your red nest. Am I your Greek,
am I your lamb, your namby-pamby boy
back from poppied isles, or just another
suitor in your deck of bards? That moan-song
I hear behind the wall at night—you turn
from tonight's pal to face the wall, make sure
I hear each sour note you pour in my ear
through bricks of mud and loam: that song's for me.

SONNET WITH RAIN DANCE AND GITANES

Jealous of the one who does not exist,
never the one who does. *Him*? His dirty
Peugeot parked where you thought I wouldn't see
his pack of French cigarettes on the dash
as I walked home on Grant? The mandolin
picker with his beach house? Who cares about
them? But the one with iridescent wings
on his cock, the five octaves he can sing
with it, the one whose dancing calls forth five
forms of precipitation, from drizzle
to downpour to hail, and each more wanton
than the last, on the parched grass where you live.
I've never seen him but know he exists,
as the Devil howls and knows God exists.

SONNET WITH TWO MAGGIES
AND A RIVERBOAT

You're the Maggie May who wrecked Rod Stewart's bed
and the Maggie who made Dylan scrub
the floor. You're the Mustang Sally who'd ride
with Buddy Guy, and you're Suzanne in rags.
You're Long Tall Sally who's got everything
Uncle John needs, and Proud Mary who hitched
a ride on Tina Turner's riverboat
queen. Hello Dolly and Goodnight Irene.
You're the one in a flared red dress, crawling
up Patti Smith's stairs. Knock upon her door.
She's true to you, lamb. Now tell her your name.
Have mercy on her. You who take away
the sins of the world, *tell her your name.* And
your name is G . . . L . . . O . . . R . . . I-ai-ai . . .

SONNET WITH ZIPPER
AND BIOLUMINESCENCE

What cut was how comfortable you were
telling me about him—*I've never been so*
excited—how he unzipped your cutoffs
as you cuddled. A boy so young you could
show him not just the ropes but the rigging,
sheet and mainsail, jib and spar, then come back
to tell me all about it: the blue earth,
sun and stars revolving, clock that creates
the very time it keeps. You did it all:
the winch, the wheel, the sextant, celestial
navigation. With him you saw the red
tide and a redder sunrise. And you came
back and described it to me. I listened.
I got it. No wonder I married you.

SONNET WITH PURGATORY AND SCRATCH

Just once you let yourself go, just enough
to let me know what I was missing all
the other times. The *you* you let go flowed
out of the you who let go; the jazz band
leader cued the alto sax to solo,
take all the time she wants. You played the hell
out of that tune, turned it into a blue
velvet purgatory, a river born
squalling from a river, more beautiful
than any heaven's harp plinking a fugue.
You did it to my percussion, dovetailed
my rhythm. It was my snare and my steel
pans, my glass harp and gutbucket. To my
brush and scratch you kept such smooth time, one time.

SONNET WITH BARK AND FLOOD

Hetch Hetchy's Wapama Falls, its nonstop
drop and then the 600-foot cascade
past blue lupine and manzanita's red
bark: I've seen you *be* that. Be ten thousand
monarchs roosting in eucalyptus trees,
sucking the pink stamens' nectar, their sense
of taste a hundred times stronger than ours.
You want all the sugar, not just the cane.
I've seen you be the night sky, its paltry
display of visible stars suggesting
the septillions we can't see. I was waiting
for an outburst or nova but it's
your roaring *in*-burst that inundated
everything I'd ever known in its light.

SONNET WITH LAVENDER AND CHOWDER

Those who spend years in silence, milking goats,
listening to water flow underground,
know something I don't, rare as lavender
pearls in chowder. Do the weird harmonies
of matin song evolve, as the faithful
believe, from orisons of frost, or does
the music prove what seems unbearable—
that humans are as far from nature's grace
as Verdi's *Requiem* is from the soft
percussion of a pine branch as it scuffs
my windowpane? Yes, they know. Those who spend
years in silence know how alone I am,
for they are more alone, though I suspect
they also know a swank, swaggering joy.

SONNET WITH GOLDFINCH AND PEAT

Does the red maple consider the finch
perched on its top branch, the complexity
of her gold-black wings, her ability
to fly away? It's one of so many
relationships where only one party
has the power to leave. And does the finch
consider the maple, how it takes root
everywhere from pure granite to peat bog—
no urge to explore other earth, to splurge
its scarlet on a distant hill? I can't
ask you to share yourself with only me,
no more than you could ask to be a book's
one reader. But how fiercely the pages
would blaze in your solitary fire!

SONNET WITH GHOST WRITER
AND SYRINGE

Who is that angel in Bernini's white
marble of St. Teresa? He's so strange:
her ecstatic communion is with God,
not him, the winged sous chef who'll tenderize
her flesh for the Master to come, a ghost
writer who'll never get the credit or
the girl, and won't mind. He holds his arrow
as lightly as an afterthought, no blood
or viscera, lifts her disheveled gown
like a pusher about to pierce the skin
with such skill she'll feel just the aftermath:
sudden, shooting warmth. His beatific
grin is because he knows her real bliss
will come now, with him, not after, with Him.

SONNET WITH POST-ITS AND JOHNNY DEPP

I grubbed through every Post-it in your trash,
puzzling them together to find the place.
I hopped an Uber, snuck in the lobby,
tried to make sense of the words on the wall.
Dentists, tailors, an actors' studio,
vacant. What did I expect? Rendezvous
with Johnny Depp? What would you see in him?
Index as: "Sensitive, he's so." Edward
Scissorhands, boohoo. I want *his* secret,
not yours. He knows the reason he is loved
is not that he's gentle or good. He knows
his huge ice sculptures are kitsch, their saving
grace the shavings shed in their creation
and falling, falling, all over Burbank.

SONNET WITH ABALONE AND GLUE

You say it doesn't mean a blessed thing,
but don't you see—that's what I want. That's what
I envy. The ocean ebbs, revealing
blue anemones, yellow barnacles,
a lone iridescent abalone.
It feels nothing for the moon, whose being
transformed it into this revelation
in tide pools. What human being would say
it means nothing? What it means is the most
blessed thing imaginable. The hide
of a noble horse becomes glue that holds
the ribs of Itzhak Perlman's violin
as it sings Mozart and Rachmaninoff.
Tell me what he does to you means nothing.

SONNET WITH BLIZZARD
AND GLASS LIZARD

Homo amator: the species that loves
and so makes symbols. Shoot: I don't just win
if I roll a natural, I'm an ace.
Love: if you want me, all of space and time
wants me. Jesus wants me. The glass lizard
in the Louisiana piney woods
wants me. El Niño wants me, brings me gifts
of blizzard and rain, and the Peony
Nebula wants me to rout its red clouds.
But when you don't? My dice turn to snake eyes,
a plague of hail pelts my block, and Jesus
doesn't want me in Zion. He's lost
in a book that shuts when I come near. Your shot
silk pages open at his touch alone.

SONNET WITH ICE HOCKEY
AND NIGHT GOGGLES

Who are you with now? Maybe some jarhead
or SEAL, the guy who slid down a thick rope
from a Black Hawk one moonless night and shot
bin Laden. You love when he wears the night
goggles. Or maybe Mario Lemieux,
six feet, four inches of hockey genius,
Montreal grace and Pittsburgh grit. Isn't
what I'm afraid of that you're with my dad,
saluting the dashing Dr. Thomas,
Navy captain and surgeon, authorized
to operate on a nuclear sub
in case of World War III? I can see you:
brave nurse, longing to hand him his scalpel,
how flawlessly his hands open the flesh.

SONNET WITH VENISON AND FRIGG

Are you still reading that book? Karl. Ove.
Knausgaard. He's hitchhiking on a narrow
highway above the fjords: you pick him up.
He's eating venison and chips alone
in the corner of a pub: you join him
and discuss what it is about eating
in the dark—it's so *northern*, eating fire.
How can I compete with his rough-hewn looks?
For Frigg's sake, how can I hope to survive
my struggle with a man with a double-
voweled name? While I polish my language
with lambskin and linseed oil, you're gutted
by his wild syntax, his rugged diction
cutting your hand as you dog-ear the page.

SONNET WITH STORM DRAIN AND THYME

If I can't have you, I won't have another.
Torrents and trickles mix in the storm drain,
but each splash wants to be cherished. One has
just one mother. If she doesn't love you,
Sister Susanna's interest in your cute sketch
of your Scottie is watery milk.
Your sweet muck can flood the Suck Street gutter
for all I care. Gush, honey, share it all,
underground and straight to the sea. You taunt
and haunt; still I want your dirty water.
Without you, sure, I would still have dusk clouds
engorged with gorgeous rose and melon light,
black bean soup with thyme, and the warm wood stairs
that lead to my awful and quiet room.

SONNET WITH TWO TORCHES
AND ONE CLIFF

Are the divers off La Quebrada
rehearsing their death or just paying the rent?
They need to calibrate the tides to make sure
the water is deep enough. They need
to take both space and time into account.
Death is cold, but that turbulent sea
can almost reach body temperature. I think,
my love, you love that boy who risks breaking
his graceful body into a million
brilliant scintillae. So I imagine—
rehearsing losing you. The night diver
raises two torches in his outstretched arms,
bundled sticks soaked in wax, sulfur, and lime
so their flames keep burning underwater.

SONNET WITH FISH AND BAYONET

I can't forget seeing them share the sole
through the window of Tadich Grill, someone
I don't like, daring to split a carafe
with someone else I don't like. Am I that
shallow? And yet the way she lifts her glass
like Liberté: red flag and bayonet.
As if I'd never learned of endangered
species, including mine, or heard of lead
in drinking water. Never seen the brusque,
middle-aged mother with no way to know
if anyone will look out for her child,
now playing hide-and-seek so happily,
as the sun goes down behind the pear tree,
in the tool shed where the sharp things are stored.

SONNET WITH EARTHQUAKE
   AND VERMOUTH

Trapped in your glass tower after the quake,
you imagined me walking miles through dust
to see if *she* was all right. I in fact
was searching for a bar with a payphone
to see if you were. Smell of sweet vermouth
and maraschino cherries in a back
hall that's heard more than its share. Was it so
hard to believe that someone loved you? Not
that it was impossible I'd rub knees
with some record store clerk. You and I share
our sheer ignorance. What we're sure is shit
is the most precious thing in us, the slick
pit we spit out. Funny phrase. Talk to me, .
love, tell me what hurts, what thrills. *Spit it out.*

SONNET WITH BLUE SPHERE
AND RUBY, MY DEAR

If only you were in love with quasars
and their staggering luminosity,
or a hummingbird, attuning yourself
to its three thousand wingbeats per minute—
how could I compare as you thrashed yourself
into lather? Or music, but even
the spherical chords of Thelonious
Sphere Monk—even they are, finally, born
of human hands that caress inhuman
instruments. What gets me is that the one
you want has blood like mine, though in the heat
of August he can sense the coming fall
and 'round midnight he is as unlike me
as a prism is from a straight white line.

SONNET WITH HAM AND ROSE

I see God as a sort of rectangle
of rose light, and the light is paper-thin—
slices of ham at the deli that fall
into the butcher's big hand from his steel
machine. Not that I *believe* in that sheer
page of light, but that's how I imagine
those who've seen God see everything: the pots
on the range, clouds, streets with garbage cans
at random intervals, silent at dawn
before the truck's high-pitched whine. I envy
those who see it. For me to deny it
would be as if one with no sense of touch
denied the existence of fire to Jeanne d'Arc
as her face shone in the flames' light.

SONNET WITH MUD AND PILLOW

Was Iago jealous of Desdemona
or, instead, was he jealous of the depth
of Othello's love? Iago thought he just
wanted a new job—so much like us, not
knowing his true desire. His jealousy
sloshed its muddy path into Othello.
My God, it must have been so hard for him
to smother her with a pillow. Did he
shroud her eyes, or watch them fill with the tears
that fell from his own as he strangled her?
What he saw there was awful and tender.
He could see that even then she knew him
better than anyone—she loved him and
no one else—even as he finished it.

SONNET WITH JUICER AND PRISM

Oh, you are gorgeous, yet you give yourself
to that cobless corn silk, that vegetable
juicer of a man. Why? Because you can.
Your power flares out exponentially
when you do, like a peacock's train. You give
your love not at your whim but at your will,
just as God gave himself to Bethlehem,
for no reason, as a god would, and like
a peacock's train your royal robes glow not
from their own pigment but geometry:
each plume a web of microscopic prisms.
You are the *I Am* who grants him your love,
and he blooms as you groom him for your grove,
staking him erect in his wire mesh cage.

SONNET WITH EMERGENCY ROOM
AND SKILLET

The three of us got back from the ER
and popped corn. Your roommate had cut the bulb
of her thumb, that most and least erotic
zone. She was afraid that later that night
we might fool around unless she went us
one better, and it worked, and we cooked it
in a cast-iron skillet—lots of butter.
She'd used a fancy pair of poultry shears
and flirted with the doc. What did she think
we'd do behind the chipped paint of your door,
witnessed only by your mute blue blanket?
She didn't want me, or you, but a third
thing we didn't have, though we smacked of it.
No one is ever loved as they deserve.

SONNET WITH USED CAR AND JULIA CHILD

You were there with *him*, weren't you? I knew it.
He knew how to order wine. The quiet
chianti that left red welts on your tongue.
He knew you better; he loved you better.
He knew how to put you back together
after the deboning, like Julia Child
did with a Thanksgiving turkey: no one
could tell it wasn't whole. You would love him
for that. No you now. Just scraps. Ecstatic.
After lunch he took you to buy a car,
got you a deal that made you cry *Olé!*,
the dealer dripping blood from wounds so clean
he hadn't felt a thing. You were banging
all down the road like cans at a wedding.

SONNET WITH LAMB AND LAST JUDGMENT

The first girl to give birth must have asked herself:
What is this slippery flood of lamb
or lion lunging out of me? God sees
us as we are on Judgment Day. I'll be
revealed as this bloody squall I've hidden
inside for so long. Once it's born and looks
around, it thinks: *All I was so sure of*
was wrong. Or is it me who sings that song?
As lost as he must be, I am. Will be.
I made this flesh with eyes that can see me.
I can love him or go blind. Love, you look
like the precious part of me you came from.
The world adores in you what it reviles
in me: this red, wet, wrinkled mystery.

SONNET WITH SIGN
AND ROMANSCH LANGUAGES

That hotel maid who didn't speak English
or even Spanish—remember her? You
were fifteen. It was Romansch, from the Alps.
Your parents had gone to dinner. She made
the bed, tucking the sheets with what your mom
called hospital corners, then sat firmly
at its foot, patted the quilt, inviting
you to join her. What did you do? Played dumb
(*were* dumb), shrugged your eyes as if not knowing
what her mouth meant. The adorable
(literally) freckles on the slopes of her breasts
faded into the pinkest blush—sunset
on snow—you'd ever seen. You must forgive
yourself for what you didn't do—she did.

SONNET WITH WARM MILK AND SHOVEL

The final, excruciating envy
is of those with faith. The burden of proof
is not on them. *Tell me who I am, Lord,*
and a voice intones: Arise, go heat milk
for your morning coffee. Shovel last night's
snow off the driveway. Listen to the rasp
of scraping snow and how it differs from
the blade's ring on concrete. That's who you are:
the one who warms the milk and shifts the snow.
It's not simple to live simply. You can't
do it. Thomas needs to see the body
open to know he's loved. But his question
is whether *he* can love. Another's scars
will never be enough. He doubts himself.

SONNET WITH TOOTHPICK
AND STREET FAIR

At the Telegraph street fair Hank's cousin
Denise got me lemonade with a slice
of Key lime, and when she gave it to me,
she gave me a truckload of shot-in-the-arm.
She gave me time she gave me space she gave
me a red, white and blue earthquake and Lord
she knew what she was doing. I barely
knew her and it wasn't sexual but
she gave me her body and her soul and
more than I've ever wanted anything
I wanted to *be* her, to be someone
who could do anything so completely.
The toothpick that stuck in the plastic cup
pierced the sky and it came down, here and there.

SONNET WITH CLERK AND GENGHIS KHAN

Of course there are the Caesars and the Khans,
the ones who leave their mark, often in blood,
great swaths of it over the plains and moors
and tundra. Others leave a lighter mark:
pastel, pen, plume. What I don't understand
are the anti-Khans, the man who wishes
he could have vanished in the smoke that curled
from the ash of his grandmother's letters
to an office clerk. Not mere love letters
but letters that would cut steel, show the blind
the Milky Way, a/k/a Winter Street,
Path of Cranes, the Road to Santiago.
Someone who would burn those words must believe
the aroma would bring God to his knees.

SONNET WITH AIOLI AND ROUX

The chef, of course it was the chef. You can't
resist someone who *knows*: when to simmer
and when to poach, how hard to whip the roux
(mercilessly), how to fold the foaming
whites into the soufflé (ethereally),
his pudgy fingers perfect for a pinch
of cardamom, a dash of mace. He whisks
the olive oil till it emulsifies
and turns to aioli. You make a noise
that sounds like *aioli*, a euphoric
lament for all us lonely shlubs and grubs,
pale, wingless, who roam the orchard, dewy
apples out of reach. Still, to overhear
your love may be as good as tasting it.

SONNET WITH SWAN AND LONG TALL SALLY

What if we're the crux, the diamond linchpin?
What if creatures in other galaxies
have a vague sense that something is missing,
but don't know it's Little Richard, Shakespeare,
and cornbread with plum jam? They have their songs,
but like the Rolling Stones' *Voodoo Lounge*, not
Exile on Main Street, or as if Monet
stopped painting before the water lilies;
their idea of sex is what dogs do or
Nixons. Their squidy eyes would see the most
gauche galoot of us as Baryshnikov
dancing *Swan Lake* on gold wires, dulcimer
strings over water. And for what that dark
lake is made of, their language has no words.

SONNET WITH SPLINTERS AND VERONICAS

The loft above the garage—who would have
found us there? Among my mother's college
scrapbooks, souvenirs from her Chicago
nightclubs, her weekend escapes from Duluth.
You would have lain back on the army cot
Uncle Wally had stored there years before
along with the mess kit from his two wars.
I would have knelt on the splintered pine floor
as you put my hand on your *Hard Day's Night*
T-shirt—George looked like Jesus on the Shroud
of Turin. I'd stroke your veronica,
the veil that wiped the sweat from Jesus' skin
and the final pass of the matador's
small red cape over such gently curved horns.

SONNET WITH SLINGS AND SLIDERS

I was sure you met him for crab sliders
and gin slings at that bar on Mission Bay.
I was sure he rode in the Tour de France
and you met him on the high stone ramparts
of Carcassonne. I was sure when you talked
with him that words were used like *entropy*
and *orrery* and *roc*, then repeated
until they lost their meaning, became pure
sound, returned to you with wilder meaning.
It never crossed my mind there was no one,
no hipster you met for an IPA—
that you went home to pound cake and cable
and watched a tanker out your small window
fade softly into ordinary clouds.

SONNET WITH MAENAD AND KILN

The dancer on a Greek vase—her figure
drawn with a brush made of a single hair!
Fired three times in a limestone kiln: the first
to turn paint and clay both red, twice to turn
them black, then thrice to sunder red from black,
revealing the maenad cradling a fawn.
In the first fire all she wants is to burn
the *otherness* that keeps her from her gold,
molten love, so the soft beast can be born.
Then all is charred. She learns to dance alone,
unseen, untouched, unknown. It's the final
fire that transforms her: the turning potter's
wheel turns into her, her thirst as she whirls,
wearing the skin of the fawn she had nursed.

SONNET WITH HEDGE FUND AND TROUT

If (*when*) she gives herself to someone else,
would you want it to be your opposite
or some galoot like you, only better?
Maybe hedge fund brokers need all that loot
to compensate for their pain. If your ex
ends up with one of their kind, it's total
victory: "I *knew* you'd end up with a rich
arbitrageur." What you don't want to hear
is she's gone to Montana to shack up
with a novelist who hooked the biggest
Yellowstone Cutthroat she had ever seen,
then let it go because he loves nature.
Someone who tossed his book into her wood-
fired stove, sat down and wrote a better one.

SONNET WITH Q-TIP AND FUGUE

A man in bed lies wheezing in some pain.
His age doesn't matter—he is old now
because he is dying. He wants water;
he wants orange juice more than sex or music.
He wants someone to open the window
just enough for him to hear the pigeons
under the eaves, the shouts of the trucker
asking where to drop the box of needles.
You swab his lips with a juiced-up Q-tip
and change the horrid inspirational
organ chords the nurse picked to his beloved
pink screaming punk fugues. You begin to hope
he has reached the unimaginable
morning where he does not want another.

SONNET WITH ACNE AND HAWK

Wadsworth: the homeliest boy in homeroom.
My acne looked like the gentle foothills
of the Sierra next to his Rockies.
Kenneth, but kids (not me) called him the Wad.
Our class went on a field trip to the snow,
and I, the most romantic of the bunch,
wandered up the frozen river, giddy
screams of rowdy carousers soon eclipsed
by the softer scream of a distant hawk.
Ken came around a bend in the river,
hand in hand with Kate Dunn, her shirt open,
her breasts brazen in the pine-scented air.
No one spoke, but they had no fear, while I
was suddenly afraid of everything.

SONNET WITH INK AND GAZELLES

If one holy scroll had survived the flood,
would it be filled with visions, whitewater
ecstasies, or would the parchment, leather
dried from the hide of gazelles, marked with ink
ground from the charred bones of cattle, reveal
a more honest scripture: *Don't follow me
out here. It's not worth the sacrifice
of even one lamb. Be wise: stay by the fire.*
The saints came later, those who chose to live
on pillars of ice. We'd look from our caves,
see their glacial figures and imagine
love locked in their frozen eyes, against all
evidence, until the river of hate
flowed clear and strong and could not be denied.

SONNET WITH SCHLOCK AND YONDER

Multnomah Falls at Columbia Gorge:
the sun slants from the southwest and a gust
flares so the falls blow down from the southeast—
that *moment* when they converge in the pool
below, and we're staring into the core
of Oregon. God comes like that. Seven
seconds in Coltrane's *Love* that justify
the ways of love to man. Hardly ever
does it last that long. All the rest is schlock
and irrelevance. It was only three
seconds that I watched you taste the gravy
as it simmered and I could see your eyes
thinking hard about something and my love
went farther than the baby blue yonder.

SONNET WITH DEATH
AND RED-CHECKED TABLECLOTH

When I die, may you go to the dark place,
which is what we called that Italian joint
on El Camino, and may a waiter
handsome as the devil himself whip up
a carbonara from angelic eggs
and sea-salt-cured prosciutto made from pigs
nurtured on Parmigiano Reggiano.
May you follow him down basil-scented
halls to a storeroom, lie down on a bed
of coffee beans slick with dark roasted oils,
and forget me. At least may your memory,
if God answers any prayers, be as faint
as an old man's memory of the perfume
his mother wore as she rocked him to sleep.

SONNET WITH MOUTH AND STONE

Surely the red rhododendrons did not
evolve to pleasure us, nor the river,
its music as it smoothes rocks into stone,
nor the star-splashed sky. We must have evolved
to find pleasure in them, to make them *mean*.
Our ears must have evolved to hear water
so we could find it among all the noise
of the jungle. And the flower's crimson,
almost as if it were human, a mouth
or a throat (blue is not a human hue).
But why the night? How welcoming the void—
how like us these fires in the woods that give
each other light, if little warmth. Or else
like embers that give warmth, if little light.

SONNET WITH OVEN AND GREEN NETS

On the ground floor of the monastery,
an oven, a cistern. All that you need.
To wake before dawn and pray, then gather
the fruit where it's fallen into green nets
you've hung from olive trees. It is still dark
when you return to press the virgin oil,
whose taste is too delicate for the light
of the Tyrrhenian Sea. So you pray
to the olive, the bread, the sandal strap
torn on the path. To the lizard, waiting,
like you, for sun it doesn't know exists
and can't imagine. You pray and become
empty like them, not knowing if the path
exists, or love, or bed, or dove, or bread.

SONNET WITH PIZZA AND REVELATION

While I was listening to Steely Dan,
she listened to Sun Ra. She did know how,
though, to let down her elegant updo
when I least expected, for example
when she rose from the choir for her solo
of "Panis Angelicus." I thought then
I could talk to her about anything—
the wrack and ruin of the Trinity.
In fact she and I were a breathtaking
mismatch. We could talk about nothing. Nor
eat pizza, hook up, or listen to Liszt.
For you, my love, to be jealous of her
is like the vineyards of Revelation
being jealous of the wasteland of Job.

SONNET WITH HARVEST AND SIZZLE

The ones for whom it's enough just to be—
to plant tomato seeds, tear the harvest
from the vine, toss it in the sizzling grease,
then wait for the red sauce to thicken and
release the marrow—are they the holy
heroes who save the world? While we others—
those who want to make a difference—is that
original sin? To be unable
to drag one's foot in the river, bleeding
softly from a scrape against a stone's edge,
without needing to paint the flowing glow,
or freeze its music in a melody,
or decide whether the blood runs brightly,
secretly, brazenly, or royally . . .

SONNET WITH AURORA AND AURELIA

Tsunamis of blue, ruby and emerald
flood the earth from the west edge of Iceland
to the isles of Tierra del Fuego.
I saw it on TV: fresh video
NASA just released of the aurora.
fMRI scans show some people's brains
look like that 24/7. Maybe
their minds resemble the aurelia,
translucent jellies reflecting the ocean's
opulence that surrounds them. We forget
sometimes a reflection is more intense
than the original. That's what art is,
isn't it? The mirror's sharp edge. Echoes
whose feedback warps a croon into a screech.

SONNET WITH RUBIES AND STRIP

How I want some animal to love you
with a depth that transcends mine, as diving
into the South Yuba River—the shock
of the cold on griddle-hot skin—transcends
the equation that graphs the splash. How small
the world if my Vegas Strip magic act
were the only act in town. I long for
some brash and ruthless angel to cleave you
in his black box with a ruby-hilt sword,
work you and play you till you burst like doves
at his touch. His mammoth wings that could split
a cedar. How could I not give you up
to one who turned your water into wine,
if only that would mean that he exists?

SONNET WITH HOUND AND SEQUINS

I didn't lose you to a matador
in flat slippers and a sequined jacket.
I didn't lose you to a match's glow
you followed into a hummingbird's nest.
I didn't lose you to Bruce or Abby,
though Bruce could bawl blues like a baying hound
and Abby danced like a leaf in a storm.
I didn't lose you to a silent drum
or a curtain call or a summer sheen.
No, I lost you to incomparable
suave death in tights and tank top, his slick
disco two-step. While he took you for a spin
in his roadster, his red Alfa Spider,
I rode in the rain on the rumble seat.

SONNET WITH CRUSH AND MUSTARD

"But to lose you—to *her*!" How we relish
the mischief of the brat with the arrow,
lionize the roar of our latest crush.
When your wit whacks me back, her candor bucks
me up. Yes, her *sincerity* turns me
on. It must burn that your blonde bangs leave me
flat as a cracker while her straight black locks
leaven me, Easter bread rising with milk
and honey. Your neurosurgery numbs
my nerves; her hot mustard plaster pleasures
them royally. Your five-octave voice delves
the Everglades of grief and Everest
of desire, and all I want is her
hell-bent, single-minded, monotone moan.

SONNET WITH RIBS AND OBELISK

I wasn't stalking you. I swear I had
no idea that you and your tank top
and high-heeled flip-flops were anywhere near.
I watched you from behind an obelisk
in St. Rose Cemetery. You rode up
with him on his bike, opening the warm
wrought iron gate as the cold gold cross hung
from your neck. You were watching yourself too,
the back of your head on a graven name,
as he kissed your twelve ribs. You were at peace,
felt not desire but curiosity.
It wasn't about him. It was the sun
beholding you. You saw that you were good
the way light is good: by definition.

SONNET WITH QUARTZ AND RICE

The two-edged sword of being human and
knowing it: blades of grass never compare
themselves to an oak or look in mirrors.
I never love you more than when I watch
you look at your reflection and relish
what you see. Only a human would do
something so dirty and shrewd and divine.
When you touch me you turn me into rose
quartz clouds, into the shadow of a hawk
passing over car hoods in a gravel
parking lot, into a tired old woman
jaywalking, carrying under her arm
a bag of rice. To be loved, to be human,
is to be, not turned on, but turned *into*.

SONNET WITH TAQUERIA AND FISHTAIL

What one person can offer another
(what I can offer you) is so silly:
I make a mean burrito, but nothing
like what's in two dozen taquerias
in the Mission. What did Bob Dylan call
Jerry Garcia? A muddy river
that screams into the spheres: *that* burrito.
I can't get close, not to mention the grace
of the jaguar or the slow explosion
of hydrangeas, and that ramshackle tramp
in the bar's backwaters who jury-rigs
his bones into a man, asks you to dance,
spins you in turns so flawless and snazzy—
fishtail, sugar push, whip—Lord, what am I?

SONNET WITH ANARCHIST AND RED ONION

There was somebody you loved, wasn't there?
I know that he had bad skin and worse hair.
Of course, he was a Spanish anarchist
who made me look like a Bolshevik prude,
adjusting my pince-nez as he burned books,
relishing my burger like a bourgeois
while he bit into a raw red onion.
You loved him for not caring how his breath
smelled, for burning the sheets with his cigar.
It cuts both ways. What if I can't love you
unless you brandish a sawed-off shotgun—
what if I can't *perform* unless you *kill*—
what awful impotence: the fear that we
can only love if it's against our will.

SONNET WITH ZINC
AND RHODODENDRONS

It could be anything that brings you back:
the fender scratch when we scraped the stone wall
when we parked by the ocean, the fragrance
of onions at rest in a glazed clay bowl,
or rhododendrons—they've more an aura
than a scent. A whole white forest of them
outside our window at Sea Ranch that May
and we barely noticed. They live more now
in memory, as sometimes experience
is the shadow of its memory, and death
the acid bath the silver-coated film
endures till the image is born dripping
from its zinc sink. The one we saw in life—
wry smile, gray cocked cap—was always the ghost.

SONNET WITH DOCK AND DEPOT

If my flame were the type to chop wood
for her fire and gather water from a well
she dug herself, if she lived off the land,
maybe I'd understand when my darling,
my queen of darts, my creamboat of moonbeam,
my train to the twelfth night hold-tight depot,
my lock my key my dock my sea my knock
my plea, my white rain and my black refrain,
took her basket of biscuits down the line
to some lilac wolf pack cul-de-sac shack
and met her meat pie there. But if I see
her with him at the Whole Foods hummus bar
and she expects me to act civilized,
fat chance. This monkey's screeching in the aisle.

SONNET WITH SAPPHO
AND WRECKING YARD

I can't compete with him, Lord Rigor Mort.
He seized you the way a crane plucks a car
and dumps its steel into the wrecking-yard
crusher. Slashes of primary colors
so much more satisfying than the wisps
of teal, topaz, twilight and tumbleweed
that mean life. All I can give you is doubt,
blue notes (not major *or* minor), the chords
the sun sounds as it rises, pale, hazy,
ambiguous, watery, pubescent . . .
not his loud and garish fire of sunset,
not its crash, its drop-dead gorgeous knockout
burst. How could you resist? Even Sappho
says Helen went freely to Troy's towers.

SONNET WITH JACKHAMMER AND ACLU

I was never jealous when I was young,
too full of my callow self and lacking
imagination. It's better to know—
yes, that one who slathered orange and blue paint
not on canvas but on saw blades, ax handles
and junked cars loved you not more but better
than I could. That ACLU lawyer
whose cross of the sheriff exposed his hate
until the jury couldn't help but see.
That fireman who stayed long after the fire
to find how it started in the garage.
I never would have checked the jackhammer.
I never would have done so many things:
raised Cain, waltzed rain, baptized your open vein.

SONNET WITH JURY AND SUNSET

For the sake of argument, let's say ghosts
exist. Amazement at our ignorance
must be overwhelming, at what matters
to us and what doesn't. Whether the rain-
pocked petals fall on the stone path or on
the clover between the stones: *that* matters
to them. Does the sunset clash with the fall
foliage or echo it? Now the ghost points
to a rabbit blending into the snow
as if to say, *The soul has no army.*
Listen. Water speaks in more languages
than are known on earth; its words are clever
as a lawyer's. They may not satisfy
the jury at first, but they will prevail.

SONNET WITH LOBSTER AND PRIEST

Why is it the rule, not the exception,
for a lobster and a missionary
to fall in love, or a king and a cork?
Nothing can come of it. Evolution,
as Whitman said of death, must be different
and luckier than we thought. The priest learns
to swim and take delight in his body,
the lobster to pray on its pilgrimage
down the open road of the sea. The cork
comes to fathom the majestic power
of its silence. The god in us does not
want what we want. The king learns the patience
to wait in the cellar till the flavors
of cedar and violet bloom in his wine.

SONNET WITH SWORD AND PETTICOAT

Henry VIII composed "Greensleeves," they say,
for Anne Boleyn. Nothing but a rumor.
It wasn't while courting her he wrote it,
but after the sentence. The loveliest
song ever written: *Greensleeves was my joy. . . .*
What did she think, stepping into her red
petticoat one May morning to prepare
for execution? *He loved me in this.*
Let him see what he's losing for plain Jane,
what a royal shower of blood I am.
Men and their obsession with their *issue.*
My girl will outlive that whore's sickly son
by fifty years, and when my Henry sings
my song to her, she will know whose it is.

NEGLIGEE AND HATCHET: A SONNET CROWN

Sonnet with Blackberries and Clocks

Brambles knotted into the Klamath mist,
swamp pop on the radio, bad coffee
in a good doughnut shop: some things you love
more than me. And the guy who picked you up
when you hitchhiked to Minneapolis,
when you had to go AWOL from the sun.
The way he didn't say a word and then
he did—how the sky blushed over Utah
as if it knew you were hitting on it,
and I love that you hit on everything:
fig jam, for fuck's sake, and closets and clocks
and libraries Open 24 Hours. . . .
You love them more too, and there's real snow now
falling like secrets in the Oakland hills.

Sonnet with Sump and Sourdough

Falling like secrets in the Oakland hills,
questions clog the drains. What could I have done?
Repaired the sump pump? When the groundwater
rose and the cellar flooded from below,
not from a leak above, what could be done?
A man's supposed to do something, or else
it's bad for business, bad for every dick
everywhere, bad all round. Tell me, sweetheart,
if I am nothing but a shaggy gob
of dough, can you stand to get your hands stuck
in this warm paste, to love this sodden sponge?
And if you can, will it ferment and prove?
Scored, crusted, slashed, charred, coarse, salted, buckled,
bronzed, ridged, cracked, geological, shining.

Sonnet with Seashell and Chinatown

Bronzed, ridged, cracked, geological, shining,
God rises from the waves like Mick Jagger
and you unzip, offering your jacket
as a beach towel. You know in *Chinatown*
when Cross says people are capable of . . .
anything? That's the anything I mean.
People will give themselves to anything.
The volume's turned up on "Satisfaction":
all you want is to 86 yourself
from the warm booth in the diner of you,
your burgundy banquettes. To deep-six your
soul you'd tender yourself to a con man,
a snake who sells his own snake oil. His blue
hypnotic scales that seem to be the sea.

Sonnet with Ark and Tug

Hypnotic scales that seem to be the sea.
The pianist plays identical notes
a dozen times, evokes a dozen shades
and shifting harmonies, as the sea turns
in its bed transposing ordinary
wind into dragons. Meanwhile I'm a one-
note wonder, my earnest tug chug-chugging
through the harbor while the sky scrolls and scours
itself for stars, hard to find as sailors
in a typhoon. How fortunate they are
to die that way, drowning in God, while those
of us still here plink-plink and go unheard,
as the child's cry was unheard on the ark,
lost in all the mating howls and bellows.

Sonnet with Vespers and Machine Tools

Lost in all the mating howls and bellows,
a virginal vespers chant penetrates
the storm of noise. Of all the forms of praise,
why does God prefer music? Why not dance
or drag racing? And if it must be song,
why not blues, *Chicago* blues: loud, urban,
industrial? Machine-tool blues. God loves
the sound of the machines that make machines.
Saints praise with their bray and swagger the blast
furnace that burns like a billion suns. But
it can't drown out the *who!* of a girl's breath
as she enters the sacred limestone cave,
willfully blows out her only candle,
and descends into the cragged grotto.

Sonnet with Ochre and Aurochs

Descending into the cragged grotto,
you see that darkness affects only one
of your senses, while it frees the others.
Water dripping from rough rock onto smooth,
you and stone wrestle each other's sinews.
A mash of mud and salt and ash and rose-
ochre clay slathers and anoints your skin.
You smear your flesh against the sweating walls
until they breathe with you, until they thrum.
You have no memory of what happened there,
but something tore and changed in your body.
You wound the cavern round you like a cloak
and left a perfect image on the stone:
the wild aurochs, their sweeping, graceful horns.

Sonnet with Jokes and Car Jack

The wild aurochs, their sweeping, graceful horns—
would you dare take that form to come to me,
knowing no human could compare to you?
What's the difference, after all, between gods
and humans? If I met Aphrodite
at Kathy's for coffee, I couldn't tell
from her skin or her figure, but her jokes
would have a weird darkness, and when she said
she'd seen it all, I'd look into her eyes
and see she *had*: her ex the mechanic
whose foot was gouged in the shop when the car
jack broke, and her other lover, the man
who sunk softly in her immortal arms
as the wild, blood-glutted swine squealed victory.

Sonnet with Barn Dance and Solar Storm

As the wild, blood-glutted swine squealed victory
and thought you were his, I was conspiring
with a lunar eclipse and a solar
storm to win you back. One of them dips you
in the equinox ballroom; the other
push-pulls and whip-spins you to Battle Creek
for a barn dance on the sprung space-time floor.
It's not me you love, but that green-eyed fox
who follows me around, one of the skulk,
and the bad weather we bring, thundersnow
over Black Lake. They're in my neighborhood
and they make you crazy, in a good way.
You love me the way swans love Michigan:
you always come back for the dirty snow.

Sonnet with Squeegee and Cracker Jack

You always come back for the dirty snow,
my red raincoat and my crackerjack car,
auto row combo of kitsch and panache.
You can be yourself eating caramel corn
with me by your side watching the Yule log
on TV. Clean my glass, my oriel,
with your sweet squeegee whenever you like;
I'll furbish, refurbish, and defurbish
your furniture until it feels like home.
I mean, with me you can break any code:
dance pas de deux with a Tex-Mex sextet,
run to Rangoon with the strongman who said
I'll be back. But you're the one who came back,
negligee and hatchet in your knapsack.

Sonnet with Zombie and Zoot Suit

Negligee and hatchet in your knapsack,
you're ready for any apocalypse,
ready to gallop the pale horse bareback,
Ziploc go-bag full of Xanax and floss.
Did you think I wouldn't understand why
you'd have to choose the one who was alpha
and omega? Zydeco and acid
rock, ascot and zoot suit, Zen and Amish,
apparition and zombie. I'm just a guy
who wants a BLT, who wants you
to have whatever *Sturm und Drang* you want.
Go! I sprinkle holy water on you
with sprigs of basil. When God kisses you,
he'll taste the light mist on your parted lips.

Sonnet Without Jukebox or Fox

He'll taste the light mist on your parted lips.
He even died for you (sure-fire technique
to get you hot) but couldn't make it last.
How sheepish the good shepherd must have felt
when he nudged the stone from the tomb, slithered
out like a cat through a crack, then lit out
for some off-the-grid kibbutz where he could
lay low till the heat was off. And you fell
full tilt for his song and dance. If I knew
the secret word, you bet your life you'd see
he was only a baritone hustler,
not the blues rustler who brings the bad news
you can't hear enough. *There ain't no more fox,*
no more rock 'n' roll, girl, no more jukebox.

Sonnet with Hard Rain and Spreadsheet

No more rock 'n' roll, girl, no more jukebox,
no more two-bit Bob Dylan and the Hawks.
What if by definition your soulmate,
who keeps you up till sunrise talking songs
(Which is better: "Hard Rain" or "Idiot Wind"?),
is impossible to love, and the one
who's inarticulate as air, who sits
across from you at the Doghouse Diner
sharing her ketchup and fries in silence,
loves you with Bachian, Beyoncéan
fathomlessness. Yes her, your un-soulmate,
verifying the spread in her spreadsheet:
she loves you with Dostoyevskian fire,
the subtlety of water, depth of sky.

Sonnet with Velvet and Buck

The subtlety of water, depth of sky:
I wouldn't want you any other way.
I wouldn't want to be enough for you.
The Klamath River cannot be enough
for the salmon that leave it for the sea,
nor is that rainbow glow, at home in both
saltwater and fresh, enough for the stream.
Is acoustic guitar enough for one
who longs to raise Cain in rolling thunder?
Can talk satisfy those who hear the swing
of the ineffable? They say it can't
be put into words. It can. Even those
who just point at the buck moon feel the twinge
as their own warm, velvet antlers emerge.

Sonnet with Oak and Aspen

As your own warm, velvet antlers emerge,
you disappear into the woods and breathe
for the first time the intoxicating
night air without the salty aroma
of my skin sullying it like sea wrack,
drink from a stream without my reflection,
sniff the faint, delicious scent of white oak,
savoring the acorns—free to pick what's
sweet to *your* tongue now, sick of my harsh elm
and aspen. If there is life after death,
the question always goes, why has no one
returned to tell us? Because they're so full
of love for *something* they've forgotten us,
as full of love as deer gorged on acorns.

Sonnet with Negligee and Hatchet

Falling like secrets in the Oakland hills,
bronzed, ridged, cracked, geological, shining,
hypnotic scales that seem to be the sea.
Lost in all the mating howls and bellows,
descending into the cragged grotto,
the wild aurochs, their sweeping, graceful horns.
The wild, blood-glutted swine squeals victory,
but you always come back for the dirty snow,
negligee and hatchet in your knapsack.
I'll taste the light mist on your parted lips:
no more rock 'n' roll, girl, no more jukebox,
just subtlety of water, depth of sky.
As your own warm, velvet antlers emerge,
you're full of love as deer gorged on acorns.

NOTES

Jealous love is a traditional theme of sonnets, perhaps *the* traditional theme, so my gratitude goes first to those poets who realized its psychological and spiritual significance, from Sappho and Homer to Marcel Proust and Bessie Smith, and especially that greatest poet, Anonymous, author of the many folk ballads that explore the one theme, as Proust said, "alone worth the trouble of expressing it."

I couldn't name everyone who has read some of these poems and offered encouragement and valuable suggestions. I want to thank specifically, though, a few people who read more than their share and made invaluable suggestions, the poetry workshop I've belonged to for over 30 years: Idris Anderson, Beverly Burch, George Higgins, Julia Levine, workshop founder Diane Martin, Zack Rogow, Lisa Gluskin Stonestreet, Jeanne Wagner, and Steven Winn.

I am especially grateful to Diane Martin, Genanne Walsh, Susan Kolodny, and Lisa Gluskin Stonestreet for their insight, friendship, and encouragement over many years (and in Lisa's case for reading and helping edit the whole book).

Thanks to Gerald Costanzo, who has edited the Carnegie Mellon Poetry Series and brought so much great poetry to the world for over 50(!) years, and also to Senior Editor Cynthia Lamb and Production Manager Connie Amoroso.

Finally, thanks to Cheryl Morris, my wife, who has patiently watched me for countless hours sit in our garden scribbling with a pen or staring at the trees. I hope she knows how grateful I am and hope I give her at least a fraction of the joy and love that she gives me.